THIS IS YOUR LIFE!

by

M. FRAZIER KEABLES

THIS IS YOUR LIFE

Library of Congress Catalog Card Number - 93-83426

ISBN 0-9630779-4-5

Manufactured in the United States of America
First Printing 1993

Published 1993
PPC BOOKS
Westport, CT

DEDICATION

I dedicate this book to my caring and unselfish Mother, Bessie Pearl (Robinson) Keables Frazier who set me on the track of investigating and testing all philosophies, religions and knowledge.

It has been a lifetime of research, but rewarding, as I found my horizons enlarging, and my goals re-defined.

To my Mother then, who wanted nothing for herself, but delighted in the enlightenment of others (especially her two sons), my belated gratitude.

ACKNOWLEDGMENT

Herewith due recognition to my wife, Elizabeth, for her intuitive guidance, her invaluable assistance and her timely suggestions. Her confidence in me is always spurring my latent talents.

FOREWORD

This book is not written by a professor, a doctor, a psychologist or a clergyman, but by a real down-to-earth student of human behavior.

It is written to reach those who have somehow not benefitted by the vast numbers of self-help books that are out there now, and for my readers to savor the wisdom of some of the foremost thinkers of this century, and of ages past.

Just what are the arts we need to master for a successful life?

In random order they are the art of communication, the art of making love, the art of sensing another's need, the art of the appreciation of beauty, the art of making others feel at ease, the art of employing our talents to the fullest, and the art of developing our individual worth.

I am sure that you would agree that to do this would be Successful Living.

As with you, forever the desire has burned in my heart for better things, better health, a better way of living, better education, a better home, a more satisfying lovelife, more trips and vacations --- in other words, the GOOD LIFE!

Since "God is no respecter of persons" (Acts 10:34), I felt there was no reason in God's world why I shouldn't have this kind of life.

Now on into the Introduction . . . .

INTRODUCTION

You are no doubt asking, why should there be even one more book written on how to live your life, and just who is this so-called expert who is going to guide me into a so-called Utopia?

Good questions.

As you are well aware, innumerable and excellent books and tapes are out there containing wonderful, wise and witty truisms. Some are very deep and sacrosanct; some are light-hearted and full of ginger; and some are mystical and occult.

How can this book be of any more value to me than any of these?

You be the judge.

I am not quarreling with anyone whose philosophical system has made anyone rich, or eased the cares of another. Admittedly, they all have a sure-fire course for some, but the big question is: Will it work for *me*?

Many of you have read the glowing testimonials which appear in each book. And you feel that you are just as deserving as anyone else, and you are! (Perhaps, even more so).

The remarkable thing to make clear right now is that "deserving" has nothing to do with it. That is fallacy #1. Get that idea out of your head.

Don't you think that I felt deserving after working a 6-day week, and dedicating myself so diligently to the task that vacations were practically non-existent?

But calendar years mean nothing in the cosmic plan for success. It is finding the FORMULA which is the trick.

And I was determined to find it!

Scores and scores of self-help and occult books I read. Hundreds of affirmations I declared; visualizing I practiced and actions I took, but there was no apparent lessening of adverse conditions.

I am not casting any aspersions on any of these books. They are all good, and I know that many of them have worked for thousands of people. Numerous authors are enlightened scholars who have given years of research to their works. Some have spent thousands of dollars on travel seeking out valuable secrets of the Eastern religions. Read these books. You will learn a great deal from them. Set yourself a program of inspirational reading. It will widen your viewpoints and expand your horizons. Thousands have been successful in working the different techniques presented. But many other thousands have been frustrated and turned off for lack of results.

Therefore, I am addressing this book mainly to those of you who have sincerely tried, but found whatever method you have investigated sadly lacking.

For years I put off writing this book, for I thought that I must have the perfect answer before putting my words into print. I pictured myself writing from a lavish studio, in a comfortable, big house in the suburbs where I would find much inspiration to write amid pleasant and supportive surroundings.

After many years rolled by and that didn't happen, I finally decided that I would start writing anyway, while still in the midst of poverty, and withal still thousands of dollars in debt.

I knew that if I were ever to get this book out of limbo it would have to be done before I had all the answers. In fact, it might even be more valuable that way. Because as my success would become more apparent, and as the different steps would unfold, then that unfolding would be of much more value to the reader.

Only by living the experience can I hope to make the knowledge in this book of worth to you so that you may profit from it. With such a variety of philosophies and systems presented by the many books and tapes on the market, how is one to know what to choose?

From the wisdom of modern and ancient sages, and from my own gleanings, I have selected those subjects which would be easiest for all to assimilate and understand, and the most effective in improving your life.

We need go no further than the Bible to find the greatest wisdom, and we shall be returning to some of its significant gems as we proceed through each of the following fascinating chapters.

Open the first chapter with joy in your heart, for a whole new world is opening up for you.

Believe it!

THIS IS YOUR LIFE!

CONTENTS

CHAPTER I
JUST WHAT IS MY PLACE IN LIFE ANYWAY?

This *is* your life . . . *here and now*!

In this book we, you and I, are going on a journey of exploration. An exploration into the Truths which you have heard about over the years, and surely have wondered about, but for one reason or another you have never applied them to your own life; Truths which I have found to be of inestimable value.

It is the author's intent to make this an enjoyable and rewarding journey, a journey to the ports of wisdom, knowledge and understanding.

This eternal question, "What is my place in life", has baffled every thoughtful man from time immemorial.

For starters, let's go to the Bible, and to some of the other eminent sages, to see if we can find some definitive answers.

Schopenauer has said, "We spend ¾ths of our lives trying to be like other people." Think about it! Three-fourths, 75%, of our existence to imitate others!

But, -- we are not like other people. We are UNIQUE -- every last one of us.

All we have to do is to observe the infinite designs of snowflakes, the numberless varieties of aquatic life and the indescribable diversification of flora and fauna we see all around us, to behold the overwhelming evidence of an inexhaustible Creator. What an array -- all pointing to individual uniqueness!

Think of that!

To succeed in life, we do not have to be like other people, nor should we want to be.

We, you and I, are different from any other creature in the universe. And how thankful we should be that we are!

Don't we realize that God does not want us to be like other people either, or He would have made us like some of these other people!

And, let's everlastingly thank God that He didn't!

In the general run of things, however, how difficult it is to strike out for ourselves, and to discover our own special talents; the use of which can not only bless us, but benefit the little world surrounding us, and mayhap go way beyond our limited expectations.

Just WHY do we copy, instead of being original?

Because it is much easier to go along with the crowd, (and we fear to be different). To prove as to why we are here; or who we really are, is too overwhelming for most of us. Not one man in 100,000 chooses to be really different from his fellowman.

But, we DO have a choice, you know.

In Deuteronomy 30-19 is the admonition: "I call Heaven and earth to record this day against you, that I (God) have set before you life and death, blessing and cursing; therefore choose Life that both thou and thy seed shall live." In other words, choose those things which will enrich and expand your life, and you will be rewarded accordingly.

Isn't it clear that this is a definite and wise choice?

There is no doubt in my mind that we are here to fulfill a mission. Finding that mission can be a lifelong quest.

But, it needn't be, and it shouldn't be.

This is where meditation comes in.

To receive this inner guidance, we must ask our Divine Source to direct us. If we are not used to doing this, it will take developing a faith we may not have at present, but it is vitally important to get on the right track.

If we can even begin to feel inside that we are starting to head in the right direction, we will save ourselves a great deal of pain and regret later on.

Setting down goals and achieving even a few of them, will definitely aid us in finding that true place which is ours alone. Rest assured, our true place is a place of happiness; it is a place of fulfillment.

And that "Place" is HERE AND NOW!

To find our rightful place, (and believe me there is a rightful place for each and every one of us) takes retrospection.

All of the above is my strong conviction, and it is supported by recognized philosophers who have done tons more research on this subject and are much more erudite than I.

Yes, being quiet, meditating and listening to your inner feelings are proven methods for putting you on the right track.

Now, you will ask, "How will I know when I have found, or am finding, my rightful place in life?"

Look for the mornings to be brighter when you wake up. Look for more satisfaction from your work, even though for the present, you may be working at an intolerable job. You will find yourself smiling oftener, and little irritations won't bother you as much.

Having a purpose in life will begin to give you more direction and more balance.

BALANCE -- there's a key word: Whether we think about it, or not, we are balancing things all of the time. We are balancing our job against our time off; we are balancing family obligations against individual desires; we are balancing time for reflection against time for recreation.

It is the KEY WORD TO A Successful Life.

As we gain a better perspective, we know that we shall not be thrown off *balance* by minor, or even major, troublesome events.

Here, then, are the essentials of meditation; a practice which will put you on the true road to happiness.

And here is the method, as outlined by DR. ROBERT ANTHONY in his best-selling book, "THE ULTIMATE SECRETS OF TOTAL SELFCONFIDENCE." *(Berkley Pub., $3.95.)*

    #1. "Relax and let go." Really relax and let your mind become a vacuum . . . . Let whatever thoughts do come to mind pass through effortlessly.

#2. "Reach out and listen." How many of us really listen? Listen for "that still, small voice"? If you hear nothing, that's all right, too. You don't expect to hear anything right away. After you have listened for a few minutes, then

#3. "Visualize and Affirm. Imagine, Visualize, Picture the thing you want. AFFIRM that you ALREADY have it!" [1] (end of quote).

I heartily recommend Dr. Anthony's book to all of you. In it he not only spells out the finely tuned details of meditation, but also cites the beneficial results, which he calls "side effects".

In your morning meditations try and sit in the same chair. You will find that it will have a magnetism for you.

Proverbs 4:13 tells us: "Take fast hold of instruction; let her not go; keep her, for she is thy Life."

And Proverbs 8:35: "For whoso findeth me (wisdom) findeth life, and shall obtain favour of the Lord." "For the words of the Law ARE your life."

Finally, "He hath showed thee, O man, what is good.

And what doth the Lord require of thee, but to do justly, and to love mercy, and to walk humbly with thy God?" (Micah: 6:8)

"For My yoke is easy, and My burden is light." (Mat. 11:30)

THIS IS YOUR LIFE!

CHAPTER II
Part 1

HOW FAR DO I WANT TO GO?

Most of us resist change. This is perfectly natural. We like the security of established habits and outlook. To counteract this resistance, think of change as adventure, as challenge, as REGENERATION!

In changing my concepts about myself, how far do I want to go?

Any make-over plan will take time, effort and concentration.

We are all in different family situations.

Perhaps your time is taken up with children, or with other household chores.

Whatever, you will have to suit your goals to your own time and pace. There are not many of us so ascetic that we can break away from all society and family to accomplish a more compensating quality of life.

NOR WOULD THIS BE DESIRABLE.

We have to modify the time and the means to achieving our goals according to family and business demands; all the while shooting for more study and demonstration within reason.

I am a great believer in family first, so I would not recommend any program which would alienate husband, wife, or other close associates.

The ultimate purpose is always to harmonize all things, all people, within your world.

You will need to find time for meditation. Get up a few minutes earlier in the morning. It will pay big dividends.
"Only as high as I can reach can I grow,
    Only as far as I seek can I go,
Only as deep as I look can I see,
    Only as much as I dream can I be."

CHAPTER II
Part 2

WHAT KIND OF DECISIONS DO I WANT
TO MAKE TO GET THERE?

Since the decisions we make are going to govern the kind of life we lead, we most certainly should not make hasty ones. However, it seems to be human nature to do so, for we all make decisions which we live to regret later on.

Since our decisions can make us, or break us, it is vitally important that we consider ALL decisions.

In my own case, at the age of 22, I made a decision which changed my entire life.

I did not know it at the time, of course, and did not realize in any way how strapped I would be for years to come.

Because of financial obligations incurred by this decision I could not get out from under the hampering vise of debt, no matter how hard I tried.

Here is a brief sketch of how it happened: After working as a store clerk for 2 ½ years, I decided to make an offer to my boss to buy his fixtures, and go into business for myself at the same location. Since he was moving anyway, and I knew all the customers, I thought that I had a sure bet. With just $45. to my name, and with no idea of how to raise capital, or how to finance a business, I opened the store doors with the optimism of innocence.

This was the beginning of many heart-rending and desperate financial trials and tribulations which would last for over 40 of the 50 years that I was in business, and just because I had made a hasty decision when I was 22.

As you may have read, 1933, the year I opened my candy and greeting card store, was a time of the Great Business Depression. The banks were closed, and people were using scrip for money.

Even though my boss left a store which was losing money,

I had the unmitigated gall to think that I could survive in this unfavorable kind of business climate.

With a naive, but absolute faith in God, I felt that somehow He would prosper me.

Due to God's goodness, I survived; yes, I survived; but a little more thought beforehand, a better understanding of God's guidance, and a better knowledge of who I really was, would have saved me from years of financial deprivations.

To sum up:

ALL of your decisions are supremely important.

Whether you realize it, or not, you are making decisions all the time. Whether you decide to be a couch potato, or whether you decide to improve the precious time you have, these are all decisions.

MARY BAKER EDDY states in "Science and Health with Key to the Scriptures", "Your decisions will master you whichever direction they take." [2]

THERE'S ALWAYS A WAY

"When discouragement knocks at your door, KEEP ON!
When fear and failure stare you in the face, KEEP RIGHT ON!
When your hope looks hopeless, and every door seems closed, there's always a way, KEEP RIGHT ON KEEP-ING ON.
When doubt and uncertainty steal your Peace and your Poise, KEEP ON!
When desperate need and want fill your nights and your days, KEEP RIGHT ON!
When your best friend turns cold and your enemies get bold, there's always a way, KEEP RIGHT ON KEEP-ING ON.
When hate and resentment sting and burn, KEEP ON!
When injustice and condemnation take their turn, KEEP RIGHT ON.
When libel and slander attack you with anger, There's always a way. KEEP RIGHT ON KEEPING ON.

When the glory of God fills your heart and your soul,
KEEP ON.
When you know you are right as God sees the right,
KEEP RIGHT ON.
When success starts to break and they all say, 'You're great!'
For God's sake don't stop,
KEEP RIGHT ON KEEPING ON!!!"

PAUL MARTIN BRUNET

Remember,

THIS IS YOUR LIFE!

CHAPTER III
CREATURES OF HABIT

"Wherein thou judgest another, thou condemnest thyself, for thou that judgest doeth the same things." ST. PAUL

Visualization and affirmations are essential requirements to breaking counter-productive habits.

Seeing yourself as you want to be is the image you want to project.

Do we even realize just how much we are creatures of habit? The process is so automatic and so stealthy that I am sure that most of us do not.

Almost from infancy we begin to develop certain "traitorous" habits. These habits become such a part of us that they are difficult and seemingly impossible to change, as they have become so much a part of our nature.

But, let us remember that our TRUE nature is God-like. It follows then that we should throw out whatever habits we have picked up along life's way which do not fit into the life-character we want to become.

Know, then, that it has been scientifically proven that it takes at least 21 days to break, or change, a habit. Since we are all actors on the stage of life, we must use our imagination to feel that we already ARE that person which we want to be. We must pursue this goal relentlessly with faith, and then, all of a sudden, we will find that we have lost, or discarded, that faulty trait.

In order to break a habit, we need a new image -- a new awareness -- for without this inspiration, we won't have the constant desire to carry us through to victory.

There must be a goal -- a goal we can believe in. Start small and work up.

Sometime ago the "Buffalo News" published this epigram, "A man can fail many times, but he isn't a failure until he begins to blame somebody else."

How do we start to change these unwanted habits? For a moment picture yourself shedding all of your beliefs, and then cloaking yourself with the beliefs which you feel are right for you. Then list one habit you want to eliminate. Decide the steps you will take to eliminate it. Write all this down and refer to it daily.

For example: Here are some habits I wanted to eliminate, and the remedies I used to combat them:

#1. HABIT: Clearing my throat before speaking.

REMEDY: Speak immediately, (and go light on dairy foods).

#2. HABIT: Speaking in a non-melodious, or raspy voice.

REMEDY: Be more conscious of the way you talk, and make the effort to sound more mellow. A tape is extremely helpful in working a change. As one singing teacher used to put it: In projecting your voice, concentrate on "Lips, Teeth, Tip of the Tongue."

#3. HABIT: Not listening intently.

REMEDY: Look directly at the person speaking, and concentrate on non-distractional listening. It is rude not to give your complete attention to the speaker anyway.

#4. HABIT: Not taking a genuine interest in what the other person is saying; and not understanding (but pretending to understand) it.

REMEDY: Even though you do not agree, or fully understand, listen well to his, or her, viewpoints. This is basic courtesy anyway.

#5. HABIT: Not being confident of your own opinions or the best way to express them.

REMEDY: Believe in your own opinions, and back them up with facts.

#6. HABIT: The extremely common habit of defending yourself, or your actions, no matter what.

REMEDY: Laughing it off, or making light of whatever it is.

#7. HABIT: Answering automatically without thinking.

REMEDY: Pause and THINK before answering.

Resolve now to make no more "Value Judgments" (DR. ANTHONY) regarding other people.

Here are more helpful suggestions: Make very short term goals -- something you can reach right away without too much effort. Success in a small way will give you the impetus to attempt bigger things. For a man this might mean hanging his neckties up, or putting the toilet lid down (nobody wants to look at the water in the toilet); if you have a pet, you would not want it to drink that water. Do anything to make yourself, or someone close to you, a little happier. Sometimes it doesn't take much. Just a little thoughtfulness. How much happier a world this would be, if we all trained ourselves to happify the existence of our family and friends!

Inquire of yourself, "What habits do I want to break to achieve my short term goals?"

Take the easy ones first, and remember that it takes 21 days to replace a bad habit with a good one.

Here is a quote to reflect on at this time: "Nothing in the world can take the place of persistence. Talent will not; nothing is more common than unsuccessful men with talent. Genius will not; genius is almost commonplace. Education will not; the world is full of educated fools. Persistence and determination alone are omnipotent. The slogan, "Press On" has solved, and always will solve the problems of the human race."

Psychoanalyst ERICH FROMM was asked for a practical solution to the problem of living. "Quietness", he replied, "The experience of stillness. You have to stop in order to change direction."

THIS IS YOUR LIFE!

CHAPTER IV

USING WHAT IS AT HAND

Now that we have explored three chapters together, it is time to discover some of the more elusive attributes of Being which are not readily apparent to most of us, but which will be revealed as we read on.

First, though, we must use what is at hand.

Let us listen to ST. CATHERINE OF SIENA. She says, "To a brave man, good and bad luck are like his right hand and his left hand. He uses both."

So, let us try and make the "bad" luck work for us, instead of against us.

DR. ANTHONY says, "It is one thing to be dissatisfied with your environment, and another thing to refuse to use it to your advantage. The thing that causes us our unhappiness is this: We will not use today, because it does not suit us. This resistance to reality utterly paralyzes our power."

And to continue, "You gain immediate power to change your circumstances when for just one day you act with force on a situation in which you find yourself, whether you like the facts of it, or not. Think of yourself as standing on a step of a flight of stairs: in order to get off that step, you must use it for the purpose of moving off it."

And in the same vein, to quote WM. E. EDWARDS of "TEN DAYS TO A GREAT NEW LIFE", "This is where I am today; my only salvation lies in acting where I am. After this assertion, things change fast. The only action that can start you off to a "great new life" is the engagement of ourselves with the job at hand. The only life one can know is *Here* and *Now*! Hopeful goals for the future rise rapidly out of Full Engagement with the Present." [3]

If we diligently look around us, we all can find something in our present set-up which we can use to better ourselves.

LOOK! ACT! Don't be deterred by present appearances.

Whatever you do, enjoy doing it. Make it fun. You will find that you will do it better and you will do it with less effort.

EPICTETUS has said: "Men are disturbed, not by the things that happen, but by their opinion of the things that happen."

And HUGH MULLIGAN puts it this way: "What I do today is important because I am exchanging a day of my life for it."

DR. RALPH C. SMEDLEY, the founder of TOAST-MASTERS INTERNATIONAL, profoundly advises: "Purpose determines the goal, marks the path, and furnishes the motion power." [4]

Perhaps, like me, you have attended lectures on psychology, or success techniques, and you have thereby picked up an idea, or two, which you have attempted to incorporate into your own personality. Perhaps you have tried DALE CARNEGIE, or TOASTMASTERS INTERNATIONAL, to give you new confidence in meeting people and to develop a new awareness of your own capabilities. These courses, and similar ones, are all excellent, and are to be praised, but unless we consistently practice, and use the principles presented, we gravitate backward into our old habits of timidity.

If we are not in a position to utilize the principles we ingest, then again we seek the easier road. We do not achieve the objectives we desire, when we do not give the time, or opportunity to follow through on the essentials that we have learned.

Remember, "There exists in the structures of every one of us a phenomenal resiliency that allows us to face up to all kinds of physical and mental disorders." RENE DEBOIS (Rockefeller University Scientist, acclaimed for his biomedical research).

We must work with what we have, no matter how little it may seem. I do not know your situation as you do not know mine, but each of us has to face up to whatever circumstances life has dealt us. Use whatever is at hand to embellish your own self-esteem.

Whatever your station, THIS IS YOUR LIFE!

CHAPTER V
TIME

What is the one thing that we all have the same amount of??? You are already saying to yourself, "Is there Anything?" Although it may not seem so at first, and there are admittedly certain contradictory conditions, yet the one and only thing we all have the same amount of is -- TIME!!!

How we employ that time determines to an enormous extent our success or failure in this world.

KAY LYONS, of the "CATHOLIC NEWS" of N.Y. has said: "Yesterday is a cancelled check; tomorrow is a promissory note; today is ready cash -- use it!"

"Nothing is worth more than the value of a new day!" GOETHE

Here is a valuable prayer for EVERY new day: "This is the beginning of a new day. God has given me this day to use as I will. I can waste it, or use it for good. What I do today is important, because I am exchanging a day of my life for it. When tomorrow comes, this day will be gone forever, leaving in its place something that I have traded for it. I want it to be gain, not loss; good, not evil; success, not failure; in order that I shall not regret the price I paid for it." W. HEARTSILL WILSON

DR. ANTHONY, in his book, "THE ULTIMATE SECRETS OF TOTAL SELF-CONFIDENCE", says, "When you snatch the whip of hurry from the hand of time, you will retain self-mastery." Again, "The secret of winning is beginning. Given the emotional motivation to take command, the mechanics of achievement will follow." And most of all, "expectancy will set in motion a mighty power within you that will cause your desire to happen. To the creative mind one moment is exactly like another.

"Each minute is rich with promise, if we could only but see it." [5]

"Since when did a clock (a bit of machinery invented by the mind of man) gain ascendancy over me? That clock is there for the order of my life as a convenience, not as a whip, or a master. I am master of that clock. If I find pleasure in my day's work, I shall gain energy from it."[6] MARGERY WILSON in "DOUBLE YOUR ENERGY AND LIVE WITHOUT FATIGUE".

So, How shall we use the time allotted to us?

Whether we realize it or not, we all seek fulfillment. How to use this time so that we shall take those steps that will bring us the satisfaction of accomplishment: that is the need. That accomplishment will give us the important lift we are seeking.

Here is wisdom for all time: "Have a time and place for everything, and do everything in its time and place, and you will not only accomplish more, but have far more leisure than those who are always hurrying, as if vainly attempting to overtake the time that had been lost." TRYON EDWARDS

Write down your goals. Divide them up into short and long range attainments.

Already by reading this far, you have given some direction to your life.

Let us listen to PABLO CASALS: "Each second we live is a new and unique moment of the universe, a moment that never was before and never will be again. And what do we teach our children in school? We teach them that two and two makes four and that Paris is the Capital of France. When will we also say to each of them what they are? We should say to each of them: 'Do you know what you are? You are a marvel. You are unique. In all the world there is no other child exactly like you. In the millions of years that have passed, there has never been a child like you, and look at your body -- what a wonder it is! Your legs, your arms, your cunning fingers, the way you move. You may become a SHAKESPEARE, a MICHELAN-GELO, a BEETHOVEN. You have a capacity for anything.

Yes, you are a marvel. And when you grow up, can you then harm another who is, like you, a marvel? You must cherish one another. You must work -- we must work -- to make this world worthy of its children."

Here you begin to see the unity of the universe and learn that reverence and respect for life are essential parts of becoming a true citizen of this world.

LORD CHESTERFIELD admonishes us in this fashion: "Know the true value of time; snatch, seize, and enjoy every moment of it. No idleness, no laziness, no procrastination; never put off until tomorrow what you can do today." (I am sure that we have heard that last phrase many times).

The immortal SHAKESPEARE tells us: "O call back yesterday, bid time return."

But, it won't, and it never will....................

So, let's live fully each day as we can, and not worry about the future, for the past is gone; all we really have is the PRESENT.

THIS IS YOUR LIFE, HERE AND NOW!

CHAPTER VI

THE IMPORTANCE OF ATTITUDES

Basic to all success books published is the directive that we be positive. How do we develop this positive attitude? We do it by asserting a truth until we believe it convincingly. If repeated often enough, and convincingly enough, the subconscious mind will believe it, and as the subconscious mind accepts it, then it will begin to carry out our wishes for betterment.

A positive attitude must be nurtured until it becomes a natural part of our Being.

As we impress the subconscious deeply and regularly, the subconscious will begin to program our life in the way that we want it. Believe and Receive. Believe and Receive. These are the two important go-together words. Repeat them. Believe them.

"For it is your Father's good pleasure to give you the Kingdom."

Why is developing and maintaining a positive attitude so necessary? Because a positive attitude produces positive results, and positive results are what we want.

Can you think of Jesus as being anything less than positive? No! He knew whereof He came, and He knew his mission on the earth.

I remember talking with a man who had been put in a concentration camp during World War II. I asked him: "Could you still thank God when you were in this intolerable situation?"

His answer was very positive. "Yes, of course", he said, "I still thanked God even though I could not see any way out at the time."

His faith finally brought him freedom. And what a marvelous demonstration it was!

In his great book, "YOU HAVE ONE LIFE -- GIVE IT

YOUR BEST SHOT", RICHARD S. CLARKE says, "Your life should become a constant paean of thanksgiving." [7] *(Page 32).* Start right now thanking God for this incomparable blessing of life.

Someone has said, "When our attitude is right, our abilities reach a maximum of effectiveness, and good results inevitably follow. Those who harbor second-best attitudes are INVARIABLY second-best doers."

Most great world figures succeeded as long as they believed in their good luck and destiny.

Learn that "Nothing else matters much, not wealth, nor learning, nor even health -- without this gift of spiritual inspiration to keep *zest* in living."

And always remember that our concept of ourselves has a good deal to do with the way we feel.

RALPH WALDO EMERSON has said: "The measure of mental health is the disposition to find Good everywhere."

And MARGERY WILSON in her fascinating book, "DOUBLE YOUR ENERGY AND LIVE WITHOUT FATIGUE" *(Page 34 - 2nd par.)* has this to say: "Unless you are paid handsomely, you will find that devotion to whatever is wrong an expensive hobby. #1. It keeps your mind off the bright and the right, which you need. #2. It prevents the flow of good to you and kills it on contact. #3. It estranges people and kills their faith in your loyalty."

Being attractive means many things to many people. A positive attitude assuredly makes us attractive to ALL people.

A French philosopher has said: "The most manifest sign of wisdom is Cheerfulness." How relevant!

Some of LEO BUSCAGLIA'S wisdom is appropriate here: "See all criticism as positive, for it leads to self-evaluation. You are always free to reject it, if it is unfair, or if it does not apply to you at all." [8]

"When you get angry with someone, stop and consider all the things you like about them before you respond."

"Don't expect the other person to bring you self-esteem, growth, happiness and fulfillment. You are responsible for those yourself."

"Value yourself. The only people who appreciate a doormat are people with dirty shoes."

"Realize that you always have choices. It's up to you."

"Keep laughing. It exercises the heart and protects you from cardiac problems."

And one last one where he says, "I have dedicated every day of my life to becoming MORE!" (End of quote)

Here are four more pertinent quotes, two from ancient, and two from modern day philosophers:

"There is a good side to every situation, and when we find the good side, we automatically whip discouragement and defeat." [9] DR. ANTHONY

"Mix a little foolishness with your serious plans. It's lovely to be silly at the right moment." HORACE

"The supreme happiness of life is the conviction that we are loved." VICTOR HUGO

And from ROBIN LEACH, the TV host of "Run Away with the Rich & Famous": "Better a thousand smiles in your heart than a thousand dollars in your wallet."

Let's add one more for good measure: "The ultimate test of whether you possess a sense of humor is your reaction when someone tells you that you don't." FRANK TYLER

Here are some signposts to indicate the road to Happiness: "First, make up your mind to be happy. Happiness is often a matter of self-hypnosis. You can think yourself happy just as you can think yourself miserable. Grab all the innocent amusement that comes your way. Never miss an opportunity to have harmless fun. Find pleasure in the simple things."

"Second, make the best of your lot. Of course you don't have everything you want and things don't always pan out just right for you. Nobody is that lucky. Even the most fortunate have a few crumpled rose petals under their umpteen mattresses. The trick is to find happiness in the lot that has befallen you."

"Third, don't take yourself too seriously. Don't think that everything that happens to you is of world-shaking importance and that somehow you should be protected against the misfortunes that befall other people. Don't grow rebellious and morbid over disappointment or sorrow."

"Fourth, don't take other people too seriously. Don't let their criticisms worry you. You can't please everyone, so please yourself. Don't let your neighbors set standards for you. Be yourself, and do try to do the things that you enjoy doing, if you want to be comfortable and happy."

"Fifth, don't borrow trouble. You have to pay compound interest on that and it will bankrupt you. It's a queer thing but imaginary troubles are harder to bear than real ones. Enjoy today and let tomorrow take care of itself. And don't forget to smile!"

Let's end this chapter with this inspirational sentiment from the "OHIO MASON":

WAKE UP TO BEAUTY

"While you are still young -- and all of us are younger today than we shall ever be again -- wake up to beauty...It is lavished upon us all, rich or poor, wherever we are -- the soul-lifting beauty of a sunrise, a lovely flower, a self-respecting tree, a sun-splashed pathway, a patient river, fluffy clouds luxuriating in a freshly washed sky, a kindly face, the softened shadows nightfall paints, the myriad numbers of stars. The list is endless. Start now to become aware of beauty; let it do its magic. Try each day to make one vivid deposit of beauty in your memory bank. Make sure that you are saving something of intrinsic value for your future besides money."

THIS IS YOUR LIFE!

CHAPTER VII

INSPIRATION AND ENTHUSIASM

Here's a good question: How do I get the kind of drive to carry out the things that you recommend?

And just how do I become sufficiently inspired and enthusiastic?

First, let's look in the dictionary for the definition of these two words:

INSPIRATION: "a Divine influence directly and immediately exerted on the mind or soul of man."

ENTHUSIASM: "Excited involvement."

Look back and you will remember that whenever you were enthusiastic in the past, you had a good feeling about yourself. The two go together. As you develop a more enthusiastic attitude, you cannot help but feel better. It's automatic. And things go more smoothly when you tackle them with enthusiasm. A half-hearted person cannot be enthusiastic -- the two are not compatible.

When you are enthusiastic, you feel a wholeness of spirit. It all ties in with "Thou shalt love the Lord thy God with all thy heart, with all thy soul, and with all thy might." (Deut. 6:5). ENTHUSIASM, WHOLENESS, UNITY, these three go together.

The EXPECTATION OF GOOD! That's what we want and need. When you are enthusiastic, you have that "God-feeling." It's a good feeling, isn't it?

It's that euphoric feeling you get when you are really inspired.

As we look once again at the word ENTHUSIASM, we find that it comes from the Greek "en" and "theos" meaning in and of God.

MME. DE STAEL defines the word beautifully when she says, "The sense of the word among the Greeks signified God in us."

In my own case, I received an awareness of things psychological at an early age. When I was 12 to 14 my parents took me to what were then called "psychology" lectures. This was when "psychology" lectures were quite a novelty, but very popular at that time. Each speaker had a different pitch, but they all played to a big audience.

Then, just as today, people were seeking a better way of life, and were willing to pay the price if believable solutions were offered.

Thus I was grounded early in the field of applied thought.

An opener which one lecturer used, I remember very well. She declared that when someone asked her how she felt, she would always reply, "Fine, of course, why shouldn't I be?"

This expression made such a lasting impression on me that I immediately changed my habitual "Pretty well" to "Fine, thank you!" Even when I wasn't feeling my best, I would always answer, "Fine!" It became such an automatic habit that I would answer "Fine" even when I was sick in bed!

Try it. The very saying of it will give you a lift.

And say it with enthusiasm!

Keep this quality forever a part of your personality, for it is contagious, and not only does you good, but carries forth to those you deal with and becomes a tonic to them, too.

One author has said, "Enthusiasm can make things 1100 percent better." Even if you don't agree with this percentage, it certainly has a plus value.

In everything you do, live it up.

MARK TWAIN, when asked about his secret of success, told his listeners: "I was born excited!"

Broadcast good news, not misfortune.

It is believing that there IS a way that is of paramount importance.

EMERSON impels us to: "Assume in your imagination, as already yours, the goal you aspire to have, enter into the part ENTHUSIASTICALLY!"

We have said much more about enthusiasm than about

inspiration. The two go together. When you are inspired, you are enthusiastic. When you are enthusiastic, you are thereby inspired. When you are inspired, you feel that you ARE a part of God's creation. You feel purposeful and useful.

The great religious lecturer KATHRYN KULLMAN has said, "I believe in miracles because I believe in God."

And DR. JOSEPH MURPHY in his book "THE POWER OF YOUR SUBCONSCIOUS MIND" expresses it this way: "Remember that a miracle cannot prove that which is impossible; it is a confirmation of that which *is* possible." [10]

Say to yourself every morning, "I feel like a MILLION. I look like a MILLION. I am worth a MILLION more!"

Expect good things to happen and they will.

"What great thing would you attempt, if you knew you could not fail?" [11] ROBERT H. SCHULLER

GOETHE directs you: "What you dare to dream, dare to do."

GREATNESS

"A man is as great as the dreams he dreams
As great as the love he bears
As great as the values he redeems
As the happiness he shares.
A man is as great as the thoughts he thinks
As the worth he has attained
As the fountain at which his spirit drinks
As the insight he has gained.
A man is as great as the truth he speaks
As great as the help he gives
As great as the destiny he seeks
As great as the life he lives."

THIS IS YOUR LIFE!

CHAPTER VIII
ENERGY, POWER AND PROSPERITY

As MARGERY WILSON paraphrases it in her great book, "DOUBLE YOUR ENERGY & LIVE WITHOUT FATIGUE" *(Page 131 - 3rd par.)*, quoting from Isaiah 40:31: "But they that wait upon the Lord (the law, or how things rightfully should go) shall renew their strength; they shall mount up with wings as eagles; they shall run and not be weary; and they shall walk and not faint."

And again the above author says, "Make this resolution now: never again will I speak in defeat, of limitation, with suspicion, or for spite, or timidly. Avoid all words that you don't want to be translated into your life as personal experiences. The secret is in the power of the inner mind.

Turn from the 'law' of diminishing returns to the LAW of accruing force. It is childish, immature, ignorant, blind and animalistic to live and think in terms of punishing limits. Accept them now, if you must, but send your mind ahead of your steps into the blessed freedom of the strength, beauty and riches of the world in which you 'live, move and have your being.'

Your life will begin to change. Your body will begin to change. You shall see God in your flesh. For life and energy are mind. All change, all creation, begin with concept. Your concept is your pattern for your tomorrows. Put the world of mind before the world of material. One or the other will be the master in our lives. One is expanding and the other limiting. By treating the 'material' as the servant of the mind, we elevate it and multiply its uses." *(Page 232 - last 2 par.)*.

For "Man shall not live by bread alone, but by every word that proceedeth out of the mouth of God." Math 4:4

MURPHY surmounts this with: "Realize and know that God is all Bliss, Joy, Indescribable Beauty, Absolute Harmony, Infinite Intelligence and Boundless Love, and that He is

Omnipotent, Supreme, and the only Presence. Mentally accept that God is all these things as unhesitatingly as you accept the fact that you are alive; then you will begin to experience in your life the wonderful results of your new conviction about the Blessed God within you. You will find your health, your vitality, your business, your environment, and the world in general all changing for the better. You will begin to prosper spiritually, mentally, and materially. Your understanding and spiritual insight will grow in a wonderful way, and you will find yourself transformed into a new man." [12]

II Cor. 5:17: "Therefore if any man be in Christ, he is a new creature: old things are passed away; behold all things are become new." How little do we realize that this is our life!

Again from "DOUBLE YOUR ENERGY AND LIVE WITHOUT FATIGUE", (Page 39), "Energy flows in when inferiority flows out."

Let us now make 5 words out of the 5 letters of the word "POWER". First the

#1. "P"-- PROBLEM, then the

#2. "O"-- ORGANIZATION, sfter which the

#3. "W" -- WORK at it determinedly with

#4. "E" -- EASE, then the

#5. "R" -- RESOLUTION appears.

With this formula you will see the beginnings of your own POWER!

JAMES ALLEN says, "If you are motivated, you can achieve anything your mind conceives. All that a man achieves, and all that he fails to achieve, is the direct result of his own thoughts."

Pause and think again about the above. Repeat it to yourself and realize its impact.

To quote again our popular DR. ANTHONY who says it so well: "Creating a positive image of ourselves is CRITICAL. The subconscious works like an automatic pilot. As you change your self-image, you change your subconscious. Our basic self-image was formed when we were about 13, and many times influenced by other people's expectations of us. It is all too true that the price tag the world puts on us is just about identical to the one we put on ourselves. Belief is the thermostat that regulates what we accomplish in life. Therefore, the SIZE of our success is determined by the SIZE of our beliefs." [13]

SYDNEY SMITH declares, "Poverty is no disgrace to a man, but it is confoundedly inconvenient." Amen to that.

BOB CONKLIN in "THE DYNAMICS OF SUCCESSFUL ATTITUDES" writes, "There is only one way that you can save money, and that is to treat savings as an expense. If you pay all of your other bills first, and hope that there is some left for savings, there never will be. Security is a feeling. Saving money is the action that helps create that feeling."

If you are mathematically inclined, you might want to look at SUCCESS this way: "Success equals Directed Effort times Positive Attitudes, divided by Negative Attitude Force."

In Proverbs we read: "By humility and the fear of the Lord (the understanding of the law) are riches and honor and life."

Although the following authors word the principles a little differently, yet it all condenses to the same basics: VERNON HOWARD puts it this way: "The realization of my natural mental health brings an awareness of impending financial success." [14]

And DR. ANTHONY: "Your mental attitudes toward your money-making abilities have everything to do with your financial condition. When you believe there is a Way, you automatically convert negative energy into positive energy." [15]

From BOB CONKLIN'S "THE DYNAMICS OF SUCCESSFUL ATTITUDES" "Let us remember that the difference between successful people and people who fail, is that successful people let their thinking correct the limitations of their environment; people who fail do the opposite -- they let the limitations of their environment affect their thinking." [16]

So he says, "Write down the things you want from life and EXPECT THEM TO COME TRUE!"

Here is BOB's recipe for financial freedom:

#1. Mold your desire to be free from debt.

#2. Bless each debt and the person owed.

#3. Ask God to prosper them, and to prosper you.

#4. Ask for the right way to pay your creditors.

#5. Start paying some small debt, as you can, on your way to freedom from All debts, and

#6. No matter what your station in life, thank God for it." A spirit of thankfulness does wonders for any personality.

Say, "I'm successful -- I can do, All my Spirit wants me to.

I now am rich -- I now am strong; Healthy, Wealthy all day long."

As our good friend MURPHY says, "My Good is now flowing to me freely, joyously, unendingly."

Let us know that God supplies us with infinite resources to meet our every need.

FRANK PICARD in "UNIVERSAL SCIENCE" says, "See how much money you have, not how little. Be glad that you have that much, and be glad that you have that much to spend. If you can succeed in analyzing your circumstances without using the word 'but', you will be astounded at what will happen to your finances. Use new money whenever possible, and take good care of your money; maintain an up-to-date billfold; use dollar bills as bookmarks. Realize that nothing has the power to keep your Good from you. Know that Nothing can obstruct or delay your reaching the life style you want."

There is no "wrong" business, if it is legitimate and honorable. Wherever you are, and whatever your wage-earning activity is, if you are about God's business, then you are in your rightful place.

This does not mean to say that you should not ask for

guidance so that you may be enlightened to change your present profession to one where you feel that your talents are better employed.

Here is a definition of True Success from RALPH WALDO EMERSON: "To laugh often and much; to win the respect of intelligent people and the affection of children; to earn the appreciation of honest critics and endure the betrayal of false friends; to appreciate beauty; to find the best in others; to leave the world a bit better, whether by a healthy child, a garden patch, or a redeemed social condition; to know even one life has breathed easier because you lived. This is to have succeeded."

The Bible tells us, "If God be for us, who can be against us?"

And Ps. 34:10: "They that seek the Lord shall not want any good thing."

THIS IS YOUR LIFE!

CHAPTER IX
SELF CONFIDENCE

The best book on this subject, and one which I recommend again to all of you is DR. ANTHONY'S "THE ULTIMATE SECRETS OF SELF-CONFIDENCE".

In this book, DR. ANTHONY states, "It goes without saying that to gain Self-Confidence, we must remove self-doubt. Self-doubt is an acquired condition, and anything acquired can be dropped. Spontaneous self-confidence is there all the time, if we could but realize it. Your crown of self-confidence is ready for your discovery. Say to yourself, 'I choose to uncover my personal strength right now!' [17]

I need not obey any negative suggestions.

Do not accept your former defeat estimate of your powers.

Forget the reasons why not -- and make a list of the reasons why you can.

Declare:

1. It is my trip.
2. I have been by-passing it long enough.
3. I, and only I, can make the trip because it is a part of me.

Once more, PERSISTENCE is your best ally. Remember our quote from Chapter 3:

"Nothing in the world can take the place of persistence. Talent will not; nothing is more commonplace than unsuccessful men with talent; Genius will not. Unrewarded genius is almost universal. Education will not. The world is full of educated idiots. Persistence and determination alone are omnipotent. The slogan 'Press on' has solved, and always will solve the problems of the human race."

From VERNON HOWARD'S "WORD POWER", Page #58, "Want to be accepted? Act as if you are accepted, and you will be, regardless of what you think about it." [18]

I say without reservation that no greater wisdom can be

acquired than to learn the import of these immortal words: "For as a man *believeth* in his heart, so is he."

What about the qualities which are supposed to make us great? Let's take them one at a time:

They are: Persistence; Patience; Diligence; Kindness; Generosity; Cordiality; Sincerity; Good Humor; Open Mindedness and Faith. Keep these qualities in mind, for as we are told in Proverbs 3:13: "Happy is the man that findeth wisdom, and the man that getteth understanding."

Why not believe in your successful destiny? It is just as easy to believe in success as to believe in failure.

"So, keep hammering away at the stone of success until you cleave it in two. If you would be strong, build up a dogged faith in yourself -- your INNER self. Do not be argued into listlessness by a calendar, a clock, or anybody's idea of how, or when, things should happen, how long it should take, or who gets the credit."

"I constantly affirm that which I wish, hold it persistently in thought, concentrate all the powers of my mind upon it, and when the mind is sufficiently positive and creative, the desires held; whether it be health, money, or position, will come to me as certainly as a stone that will come to earth when kept far in the air through the attracting influence of gravitation." THE ULTIMATE SECRETS OF TOTAL SELF-CONFIDENCE, Dr. Robert Anthony, Berkley Pub. Group N.Y., N.Y. 10016.

Here is a good affirmation: "I now make myself a magnet to draw to me the conditions that I wish."

As soon as you adopt a confident air, you will be surprised how soon it will radiate to others, increasing their confidence in *your* ability.

The How to do it always comes to a person who believes that he CAN do it.

Belief is the thermostat that regulates what we accomplish in life. Believe in yourself, and things DO start happening.

BEN SWEETLAND, the author of "I CAN " and "I WILL" states unequivocally, "When a person gains a success consciousness, he just will not fail. I have never found a contradictory case." [19]

Let us also listen to TYLER HICKS: "When you imagine that you have achieved the success you desire, you release many positive forces in your life. These positive forces increase your chances for success."

Act like a professional even though you may be doing something for the first time.

As SHAKESPEARE has said, "We are all actors on the stage of life."

So, what does all of this add up to?

1. Faith in myself (which is faith in God)..."I and my Father are One."

2. Success must dominate my mind.

3. The behavior of my person is dependent upon my assumptions.

4. Financial fullness can be and is mine ALREADY.

5. The Kingdom of Expansion is within me!

6. Success is NOW!

7. Everything I need now exists NOW!

Again DR. ANTHONY advises "If the individual overcomes the basic doubt concerning himself, and his place in life, if he feels related to the world by embracing it in the act of spontaneous living, he gains strength as an individual and he gains security. That new security is dynamic, and is not based on protection, but on man's spontaneous activity. It is the security that only freedom can give. The more you have in your head, the more alive you are. And Page #209, "As you implant the seeds of confidence, in your consciousness, your success will follow. And you implant these seeds by knowing that you have the ability to do what needs to be done. Discouragement can always be overcome by the resourcefulness of your mind. This resourcefulness is *unlimited*. Use it." [20]

LA ROCHEFOUCAULD has said, "The confidence which we have in ourselves gives birth to much of that which we have in others."

Think of your victories, not your defeats.

THIS IS YOUR LIFE!

CHAPTER X

ESSENTIAL TRUTHS AND AFFIRMATIONS

ARABIAN PROVERB: "He who knows (pause) and knows he knows (pause) is wise; follow him. (pause) He who knows (pause) and knows not he knows (pause) is asleep. Wake him. (pause) He who knows not (pause) and knows not he knows not (pause) is a fool. Shun him. (pause) He who knows not, (pause) and knows he knows not (pause) is a child. Teach him."

No one says it better than DR. ANTHONY in his book, "THE ULTIMATE SECRETS OF TOTAL SELF-CONFIDENCE." QUOTE: "The degree to which you will awaken will be in direct proportion to the amount of truth you can accept about yourself." And "You can only change yourself to the degree that you become aware of your 'mistaken certainties.' *Nothing* can stop you from achieving self-confidence, if you really want to. Every decision you make and every action you take is based on your present level of awareness. You can never be better than your own self-esteem. Never forget that your Creator has given you the free will to do anything you wish within the limits of your physical and intellectual capabilities. Actions may be wise, or unwise, NEVER bad or good. There is a universal proverb which is that we are never given greater opportunities in life until we have proven that we are more capable than our present work demands. But, remember, because 'the Kingdom of Heaven is within you', you are personally endowed with the ability to choose, and the potential power to accomplish anything you desire! KNOW that you have the ability to do whatever needs to be done, whatever it is." [21]

Assimilate the feeling that "my own magnetic power is the Spirit of my life, mind, heart, and soul; without which I could not exist. Declare: I will use this power to imagine, desire, feel, believe, and REALIZE that which I desire to attract to me. This day I count my blessings. This day I refuse to pity myself. This day I am determined to use the Magnetic Power of my mind to attract to me greater good. 'I and my Father are one.' Therefore, I believe in myself. I believe that I can do anything I make up my mind to do. From this day forward I will believe, and I DO believe that I have the Power to attract all the things that will benefit me and be for my personal Good. I FIRMLY believe that I will receive an increasing abundance of money this day and every day of this year. I FIRMLY believe that my money goal is becoming a reality. I KNOW this is true; and NOTHING can change my strong, powerful and faithful conviction in this area."

Only YOU have the power to change, to redirect your thinking. Start following ST. PAUL'S advice: "Finally, brethren, whatsoever things are true, whatsoever things are honest, whatsoever things are just, whatsoever things are pure, whatsoever things are lovely, whatsoever things are of good report; if there be any virtue, and if there be any praise, think on these things." Phil. 4:8 And in proportion as you fill your mind with "these things", will you bring these qualities into your life.

An extremely effective way to use affirmations is described in detail in JAMES F. CULLINAN'S book, "HOW TO CHANGE YOURSELF & YOUR LIFE WITHOUT WILL POWER OR EFFORT!", which may be purchased for $20 by sending to FINBARR'S, 16 Turketel Road, Folkestone, Kent, England, wherein the author recommends the use of the pronoun "you" and your first name, instead of the usual "I". Make a tape of the same affirmation ten times, and play it back to yourself as often as possible while being very relaxed.

Whenever a negative thought comes to mind, replace it with a SUNSHINE thought.

Your outlook will soon reflect your improved state of mind. Find and pursue diverse interests. Then you will fill your life with new meaning.

NOW is always the accepted time to initiate a new direction.

Remember, you respond to the way you look.

DR. GERSON illustrates it this way: "Do not make competition -- 'copytition'. Put purpose first, and you are headed toward riches."

Let us listen to the wisdom of EMERSON: "To be simple is to be great."

BIG ACHIEVEMENTS COME FROM CONTROLLED THINKING.

Psychologist WILLIAM JAMES counsels: "Believe that life is worth living, and your belief will help create the fact."

And the famous LIN YUTANG: "It is not so much what you believe in that matters, as the way in which you believe it, and translate that belief into action ."

In other words, what I do today determines the kind of life I have tomorrow.

My own words add this;

"Let sorrow be incidental,

Let joy be monumental!"

Resolve: "My words shall ever cheer

Each individual here.

Youth, vitality are expressed;

Being in tune will do the rest."

(It takes both rain and sunshine to make a rainbow).

What was it LEO BUSCAGLIA said: "I have dedicated every day of my life to becoming MORE!!!" [22]

To think better about yourself, the *key* is to *pretend* to think better about yourself, and you gradually will. Soon you will make it a habit.

"Whatever deep or shallow, new or old,

If clearly thought, can be as clearly told."

Remember that "Divine Intelligence glows through you, inspires and directs you to more worthwhile goals of creative endeavor." (Good Fortune restaurant wrapper).

Here are some gems to remember:

"A smile always adds to your face value." ERMA BOM-

BECK

"He who cannot smile should not keep a shop." CHINESE PROVERB

"Good humor is the health of the soul -- sadness is poison." ART PELOZZI

As the psalmist said, "Seek wisdom, but with all thy getting, get understanding."

DR. HARRY EMERSON FOSDICK, the famous pastor of Riverside Church in New York, put it this way: "No steam or gas ever drives anything until it is conditioned. No Niagara is ever turned into light and power until it is tunneled. No life ever grows until it is focused, dedicated and disciplined."

Here are seven simple ways to begin living a more abundant, exciting, productive and rewarding life:

1. "MEMORIZE at least one great truth every day. It may be an inspiring poem, an especially helpful verse of Scripture, an affirmation or a favorite quotation. What you memorize becomes a part of your life, your character, and your future.

2. CRYSTALLIZE your goals, your aspirations, and your ambitions. Write them down and include a workable timetable for their accomplishment.

3. SPECIALIZE in some particular field of endeavor. Become an expert, and you will soon become indispensable. Become an authority, and you will inevitably become sought after.

4. NEUTRALIZE your fears, your don'ts and your anxieties through the power of prayer, meditation, and a positive mental attitude.

5. MINIMIZE your shortcomings, your liabilities and your seeming deficiencies. Because you were designed by a MASTER ARCHITECT, you are greater than you think!

6. MAXIMIZE your abilities, your talents, your potentialities and your possibilities. Accentuate your positives!

7. RECOGNIZE the good in others, the beauty of friendship, the splendor of love, and the joy of service. Train

your eyes to look for the best in others, and invariably others will see the best in you." WILLIAM ARTHUR WARD

In the Farmer's Almanac, Vol. 161, you will find this wisdom: "I am irresistibly attracting into my experience all the good things my heart desires."

Say it again, "I AM IRRESISTIBLY ATTRACTING INTO MY EXPERIENCE ALL THE GOOD THINGS MY HEART DESIRES."

Finally for this chapter, let's think about the word "sleep" in reverse. It goes this way:

"SLEEP PEELS away the cares of the day."

What a blessing that is!

On Page 44 of VERNON HOWARD'S book, "WORD POWER", we read: "The profound truth about yourself is that Nothing in life has the power to disturb you. NOTHING! If you are disturbed, it is simply because you have given people and circumstances a false power over you. Get rid of these arrogant authorities by decreeing: "I am absolutely untouchable." No one in the world has the ability to distress me." And on Page 45, "When we face reality, when we really believe that we are human beings possessed of unassailable dignity, we no longer find it necessary to dodge verbal spears which others may hurl at us...our warm understanding melts them like ice before they can penetrate."

Remember, THIS IS YOUR LIFE!

CHAPTER XI

VISUALIZATION AND REALIZATION

"First the WORD -- the mental image.

This is the mold.

Second, the FLUX. Throw your spirit around as much of the appropriated energy as you need to fill your mold.

You have only to BELIEVE -- to KNOW -- you have it, in order to give that flux time to harden, so that all may see it."

Again, from "THE ULTIMATE SECRETS OF TOTAL SELF-CONFIDENCE," I quote: "When you visualize and keep the pictures CONSTANT, action follows, because action, after all is nothing more than *Energized Thought*. Whatever your mind can conceive, believe and picture MUST become a reality for you."

From Luke 11:9 we read: "And I say unto you, ask and it shall be given you; seek and ye shall find; knock, and it shall be opened unto you."

Again DR. ANTHONY states, "The Law of Magnetic Attraction can bring you that which you picture in detail."

We are reassured as we listen again to the BIBLE promises: Matt. 21:2; "And all things whatsoever ye shall ask in prayer, BELIEVING, ye shall receive."

Mark 22: "Ask of me whatsoever thou wilt, and I will give it thee."

If we are still not convinced, John 14:14 reiterates: "If ye ask anything in my name, I will do it."

Once more quoting DR. ANTHONY, *(3rd par., Page 153)*: "Visualize your wishes as clearly as possible; not only see them, but FEEL them. They are already a reality once they have been visualized, for that is the Law of Mind."

Do you remember PROF. WILLIAM JAMES' words: "The greatest discovery of our age is that man, by changing the inner aspects of his thinking can change the outer aspects of his life."

For "The Law of mental magnetism always attracts our true wants."

Or, as ROBERT COLLIER puts it in "RICHES WITHIN YOUR REACH", "If you will put the God in you into some worthwhile endeavor, and believe in Him, you can overcome any poverty, any handicap, any untoward circumstances." [23]

Here are some guidelines from VERNON HOWARD:

1. "Fascination with my own mental make-up is the clue to broader understanding.

2. "Going forward as a personal adventure in my own best way, carries rich rewards.

3. "My daily thoughts can produce profitable transformation both within and without.

4. "As my ability grows to increasingly command circumstances, other conditions come more and more under my control.

5. "An awareness of my limitless thought-power will provide a much richer life for me.

6. "I am now aware that I have the inherent ability to choose positive and constructive thoughts and actions.

7. "The all-powerful guidances of intuition and right motives are an inspiration to greater achievement.

8. "As my freedom from negativity grows, so will my spontaneity.

9. "The excitement of finding out the great truths about self are a stimulus to my entire Being." [24]

Now you are discovering and weighing some of the attributes of Being referred to in Chapter IV.

From the Master Teacher: "Therefore I say unto you: What things soever you desire, when ye pray, BELIEVE that ye receive them, and ye shall have them."

"For God is no respecter of persons" (Acts 10:24) "And a very present help in trouble." (Psalms 46:1).

"Before they call, I will answer, and while they are yet speaking, I will hear." (Isaiah 65:24).

"Behold I am the Lord, the God of all flesh: is there

anything too hard for me?" (Jer. 32:27).

Remember "the Kingdom of God is within you" and "Thou shalt keep him in perfect peace whose mind is stayed on Thee; because he trusteth in Thee." (Isaiah 26:3).

Numbers 12:5: "I, the Lord, (the law of your subconscious mind) will make myself known to him in a vision, and will speak to him in a dream."

God who gave me the desire, will also show me how to fulfill it. There is only one Power of creation: it is the power of my deeper self. There is a Divine solution to every problem. This I know, decree, and believe! That solution appears NOW!

JESUS has said, "I am the Way, the Truth, and the Life." By understanding this passage, that this is the Way and this Way is the "Truth", and realizing that Life is eternal, you realize the deeper import of this message, and thus you see the possibility of extending your own life on earth HERE and NOW.

Through JESUS CHRIST, our great awakener, the law of magnetic attraction begins to work, as we realize more of our own potential.

What about this so-called man of God? (He who follows JESUS' precepts?)

"He shall be like a tree planted by the rivers of waters. His leaf also shall not wither, and whatsoever he doeth shall prosper." Psalm 1:3

Therefore, "Choose ye this day whom ye shall serve... make sure that you choose Happiness, Peace, Prosperity, Wisdom and Security."

Resolve to smile automatically, reflecting your happiness and gratefulness for your present state of health, for your spouse's health, for any openings, contacts, ideas, guidance and most importantly for your gift of life on this earth.

"Let your constant companions be Confidence, Peace, Faith, Love, Joy, Goodwill, Health, Happiness, Guidance, Inspiration, and Abundance." MURPHY.

Listen to LANGSTON HUGHES:
"Hold fast to dreams;
For if dreams die,
Life is a broken-winged bird
That cannot fly."

And to SAMUEL LONGFELLOW:
"The freer step, the fuller breath,
The wide horizon's grander view,
The sense of Life that knows no death;
The Life that maketh all things new!"

THIS IS YOUR LIFE!

CHAPTER XII

THE SUPERCONSCIOUS, THE CONSCIOUS, AND THE SUBCONSCIOUS MINDS

I think that we can all agree that the Superconscious Mind is God, our Creator, the all-knowing, ever-guiding, all-powerful and ever-present Source of our Being. "For in Him we live, and move, and have our Being."

We are well aware of the conscious mind as we live with it every day of our lives, and are cognizant of its presence every waking moment. The Subconscious mind is less easy to define, as it seems to be an unknown and an unrealized force, but let's think of it as the link between the Superconscious and the Conscious mind. We can use the Conscious mind to benefit or to destroy us. In order to go forward, we will need that inner guidance which comes from the Subconscious mind when we realize that it is in tune with the Superconscious. This inner guidance we have to develop -- to find -- to rely on. Some of you have had the great, good fortune to have experienced this rare sense of intuition since childhood, and use this "unspeakable" gift naturally and easily. Then there are those of us who have not had the awareness of a subconscious mind, and we have had to diligently learn how to get in touch with it.

I have to admit that I am one of the latter.

It has taken me years of study and experimentation to realize and to discover this powerful force. For those of us in this category, it takes much investigation, dedication and persistence.

In the BIBLE we find this verse: "Seek ye first the Kingdom of God and His righteousness, and all these things shall be added unto you."

And where is this Kingdom?

Fortunately, we have a clue from JESUS who said, "The Kingdom of God is within you."

So, then, we need to look within to find that celestial spark -- that Divine quality which is within all of us. How do we do this?

There is only one way. Through self-searching, prayer and meditation.

Remember this principle: "Whatever your mind can conceive, believe and picture MUST become a reality for you." *(Page 98, 1st par., T.S.C.)* As we do this, we make a great discovery. We find that we can command the subconscious, and it will faithfully carry out our orders.

But, for it to do this, we must be absolutely sincere, and we must believe in this process wholeheartedly and without reservation. If we do, we can depend upon the results which follow. To prove this to yourself, declare to your subconscious that you want to get up at 6 o'clock in the morning. Picture the clock with its hands at 6 o'clock, and be sincere and authoritative about it, and not rely on any alarm clock as a backup. You will find that you will awaken, and you will look at the clock, and it will be exactly 6 o'clock.

Now if your subconscious can do this, how many more fabulous things can it do for you! After all, it regulates all the functions of the body, so you know that it is a marvelous mechanism.

"For it is He who has made us, and not we ourselves."

DR. MURPHY defines the "Father" as the subconscious mind.

Whether you agree with this definition, or not, it is clear that the better we understand the Divine sonship of man, the better we understand the subconscious mind. By admitting that Christ is our Savior (our link with our Source) we are confessing that we believe in this Sonship; and that as far as our understanding goes, we realize the Truth of that passage, "I and my Father are ONE."

Thus we see that the Superconscious, the Conscious, and the Subconscious minds are three parts of one Whole -- One Creative, Universal, All-Encompassing Mind. Three-in-one -- a Divine

Trinity -- "Tri-Unity," clearly reminding us of another imperative statement of Jesus when asked by Thomas for the way of salvation. Said Jesus, simply: "I am the Way, the Truth and the Life!"

How profound!

Let us know that God does supply us with infinite resources to meet our every need, and that each new minute is rich with promise.

2nd Chron. 20:20 tells us "Believe in the Lord your God, so shall ye be established; believe His prophets, so shall ye prosper."

In all of this talk about Mind, let us not forget the quintessential quality of love.

In DR. ANTHONY'S "THE ULTIMATE SECRETS OF TOTAL SELF-CONFIDENCE" we read: "Love is the attracting, uniting, harmonizing FORCE of the Universe."

Since each person is an extension of everyone else, then to love oneself makes sense.

Say often, "I am growing in the consciousness of love."

Follow these directions:

    1. Go to the Superconscious Mind to get the correct guidance.

    2. Use the conscious mind to program this information into the subconscious.

    3. Command the subconscious to carry out this information.

DR. ANTHONY sums it up this way: "Anything you picture vividly in your mind will be brought forth by the subconscious, and become a reality for you.

YOU MUST SEE YOURSELF AS HAVING ACHIEVED YOUR DESIRE.

Remember, you will get what you want when you feel that you already have it.

Your present task, whatever it is, is the most important thing you have to do." [25]

THIS IS YOUR LIFE!

CHAPTER XIII
THIS IS YOUR LIFE! REJOICE IN IT!

THIS is your life. This *IS* your life. This is *YOUR* life. This is your *LIFE*!!!

No matter how you say it, the more you do say it, and BELIEVE it, the more you will realize that this miraculous, glorious and magnificient gift is yours to activate . . . . right HERE and NOW!

The moment you enter this world, you are given the greatest gift of all -- the Gift of LIFE!!! REJOICE! Nurture It; Strengthen It; Encourage It; Re-invigorate It; Value It; Protect It; and use it for Greatness, no matter how humble your station.

Job says it so well in Chapter 33:4: "The Spirit of God hath made me, and the breath of the Almighty hath given me life."

By now we have travelled through 12 chapters together. Since the number 13 has always, whether by chance or design, been a prominent factor in my life, I wanted to make this Chapter 13 my finest and, of course, the most meaningful to you.

I am sure that by now you are beginning to lead a more rewarding life, as you have found proven ways to look at life from a brighter and more positive standpoint. Don't forget to laugh . . . . laughing is so beneficial. Remember Prov. 17:22: "A merry heart doeth good like a medicine."

DO IT!

Now that you are more aware of this life of yours and how vitally important it is, still what you do with it is up to you.

Emphasizing again the BIBLE quote, "In Him we live, (that is, have vitality), and move (have dynamic energy), and have our BEING (attain completeness)." [26] This rendition from Norman Vincent Peale's "THE POWER OF POSITIVE THINKING" furnishes us with a much more meaningful interpretation.

Herein you see our entitlement to God's blessings and endowment.

Again let us read from MARGERY WILSON'S book, "DOUBLE

YOUR ENERGY AND LIVE WITHOUT FATIGUE": On Page 14 she says, "The force of life is...like a powerful presence in which 'we live and move and have our being.'" And on Page 46: "The life-force within you is always working for you. It is always building, healing, protecting, reusing the material at hand in a miraculous fashion. All it needs is a chance." Continuing on Page 18 is this wise admonition: "Choose the fine, truly, kindly, rich, sympathetic, encouraging, vigorous words that go with your new 'part.' This person would spend no time talking about sickness, weakness, failure, or disaster, or any kind of evil, if he or she could help it. (If anybody thinks this mode of procedure is just too sweet for words, just try it). You will discover that it takes all of your strength, discipline, courage and self-control to 'make it.'" [27]

From the "Ministry of Prayer" comes this affirmation: "I can do all things through the God-Power which strengthens me. Success is mine and riches are mine. Thank you, Father. I realize that my body is strengthened and renewed. I am a perfect Spiritual being. Every cell in my body is filled with radiant health and vitality. I give thanks that God's healing energy renews, rebuilds, and restores me to perfect health NOW." I rejoice in this realization, for it is a scientific fact that our body cells are being constantly renewed, with a complete renewal every seven years.

Now you know who you are, a child -- an offspring of the Ever-Present, Universal Spirit -- a creation of Love; and your purpose here on earth is how to best use your talents and abilities to create happiness for yourself and for others, on your way to be inducted into a complete understanding of the Divine Design.

ANNE MORROW LINDBERGH in her book, "GIFT FROM THE SEA" writes: "It is not the stony wilderness that cuts you off from the people you love; it is the wildness in the mind, the desert wastes in the heart through which one wanders lost, and is a stranger." [28]

We want to dispense with this "wildness" and make those "desert wastes" bloom.

Let us pause here for some rare wisdom from an American Indian Chief: "There is no quiet place in the white man's cities. No place to hear the leaves of Spring or the rustle of insect's wings...the white man does not seem to notice the air he breathes. Like a man dying for many days, he is numb to the stench. What is man without the beasts? If all the beasts were gone, men would die from great loneliness of spirit; for whatever happens to the beasts also happens to man. All things are connected. Whatever befalls the earth befalls the sons of the earth." (CHIEF SEALTH in a letter to President Franklin Pierce).

These people sensed a unity, a purpose, a comprehensiveness of all life, which most of us today cannot fathom.

"With an eye made quiet by the power of harmony, and the deep power of joy, we see into the life of things." WORDSWORTH

It is no exaggeration to declare: "God is life and love and beauty, so therefore as an expression of God, I am an expression of Life, Love and Beauty."

Proverbs 8:35: "For whoso findeth Me, (understanding) findeth Life, and shall obtain favour of the Lord."

Prov. 16:22: "Understanding is a well-spring of life unto him that hath it."

And Ps. 36:9: "For with Thee is the fountain of Life; in Thy light shall we see Light."

Hear Philosopher PLUTONIUS: "There is always a Radiance in the soul of man, untroubled, like the light in a lantern in a wild turmoil of wind and tempest."

Let us seek out that radiance. "Gladness of the heart is the life of man, and the joyfulness of a man prolongeth his days." Eccl. 30:22

"Remind yourself that only one feeling is real -- JOYFULNESS." [29] Arnold L. Patent in "YOU CAN HAVE IT ALL".

"But let all those that put their trust in Thee rejoice; let them ever shout for joy: Because thou defendest them; let them also that love thy name be joyful in Thee. For thou, Lord, wilt bless the righteous with favour; wilt thou compass him with a shield." Ps. 5: 11 & 12. What a great concept!

Keep your body cells encouraged and uplifted. Praise them -- give them a program of youth and virility, and they will build you a body that you can be eternally proud of.

It is written in Deuteronomy 12:7: "And there ye shall eat before the Lord your God, and ye shall rejoice in all that you put your hand unto; Ye and your household, wherein the Lord hath blessed thee."

Remember to: "Keep thy heart with all diligence, for out of it are the issues of life." Prov. 4:23.

And Ps. 16:11: "Thou wilt show me the path of life; in thy Presence is fullness of joy -- at Thy right hand there are pleasures forevermore." Radiance and joyfulness are the attributes of the genuine individual.

HARRY DOUGLAS SMITH writes in "INSTANTANEOUS HEALING", "Remember that there is a resistless circulation of all good things through my life, and this resistless circulation includes my body and all its rightful functions."

In John 5:26 is the eminent truth: "For as the Father hath life in Himself, so that He given to the Son to have life in Himself."

So, "Take fast hold of instruction; let her not go, keep her, for she-is-thy-life." Prov. 4:13.

In Romans 8:2 we read the uplifting passage: "For the law of the Spirit of Life in Christ Jesus hath made me free from the law of sin and death." There you can see that it is the Father's wish that you have life and have it not only "more abundantly" but more permanently.

HENRY VAN DYKE has said: "To be glad of life because it gives you the chance to love and to work and to play and to look up at the stars, to be satisfied with your possessions, but not contented with yourself, until you have made the best of them; to despise nothing in the world except falsehood and meanness; and to fear nothing except cowardice, to be governed by your admiration rather than your disgust, to covet nothing that is your neighbor's except kindness of heart and gentleness of manners; to think seldom of your enemies; often of your friends and to spend as much time as you can, with body and spirit in God's out-of-doors; these are little guideposts on the footpaths to peace. This is peace of mind."

How many seek here and seek there without any sense of fulfillment, but the above is a proven formula for your own harmony, a quality sorely needed in this hectic world of rapid transition.

Therefore, erase all the old, negative tapes and record the new, positive affirmations NOW!

God IS, therefore I AM!

ROY L. SMITH says, "Think of your life in terms of eternity, and life will begin to expand on your hands."

To expand further on this revelation, Prov. 12:28 tells us: "In the pathway of righteousness is life; and in the pathway thereof there is no death."

"For I have no pleasure in the death of him that dieth, saith the Lord; wherefore *turn* yourselves, and live ye." Ezek. 18:32. "And we know that the Son of God has come and has given us an understanding, that we may know Him who is true; and we are in Him who is true, in His Son Jesus Christ. This is the true God and eternal life."

And to reinforce this concept, Psychologist CLAUDIUS NARANJO has said: "We are a part of the Cosmos, a tide in the ocean of life, a chain in the network of processes that do not either begin or end, within the enclosure of our skins." Being in tune with the Cosmic forces of the Universe is essential to realizing the eternality of life.

As you grasp these precepts, you will find yourself expressing the ebullience of God which is all around us, though we seldom realize it.

Smile, Laugh, Dance, Sing and Shout for Joy!!!

And don't let anyone steal your thunder.

"For he that doeth the will of God abideth forever!" 1 JOHN 2:17.

THIS IS YOUR LIFE !

A direct descendant of JOHN ROBINSON, the Pastor to the Pilgrims in Holland, the author wants you to find that special individual freedom which those devout souls were seeking.

Having spent many years collecting notes from the most advanced exponents of applied psychology, and from the Scriptures, he felt intuitively impelled to write this book.

Brilliantly written, this guidebook aspires to the achievement of a more positive outlook, and calls for a demonstration of the truisms which have been handed down from the world's greatest sages.

Knowlingly, or unknowingly, we are all seeking that mental, physical and spiritual freedom which will give new purpose to our lives.

You will find this book rewarding reading no matter what station of life you are in.

BON LISANT!!!

NOTES

Chapter I
1   By permission of the author

Chapter II
2   By permission of the Board of Directors

Chapter IV
3   By permission of the publisher
4   By permission of Toastmasters International

Chapter V
5   By permission of the author
6   By permission of the publisher

Chapter VI
7   By permission of the publisher
8   By permission of the author
9   By permission of the author

Chapter VII
10   By permission of the publisher
11   By permission of the author

Chapter VIII
12   By permission of the publisher
13   By permission of the author
14   By permission of the publisher
15   By permission of the author
16   By permission of the publisher

Chapter IX
17   By permission of the author
18   By permission of the publisher
19   By permission of the publisher
20   By permission of the author

Chapter X
21   By permission of the author
22   By permission of the author

Chapter XI
23   By permission of the publisher
24   By permission of the publisher

Chapter XII
25   By permission of the author

Chapter XIII
26   By permission of the author
27   By permission of the publisher
28   By permission of the publisher
29   By permission of the author

BIBLIOGRAPHY

"DOUBLE YOUR ENERGY AND LIVE WITHOUT FATIGUE" by Margery Wilson, pub. by *Prentice-Hall, Inc.*, Englewood Cliffs, NJ 07632

"GIFT FROM THE SEA" by Anne Morrow Lindberg, pub. by *Pantheon*, div. of *Random House*, 201 E. 50th St., NY, NY 10022

"HOW TO CHANGE YOUR LIFE WITHOUT WILL POWER OR EFFORT" by James F. Cullinan, pub. by *Finbarr's*, 16 Turketel Road, Folkestone, Kent, England

"I CAN" and "I WILL" by Ben Sweetland, pub. by *Wilshire Book Co.*, 12015 Sherman Road, N. Hollywood, CA 91605

"LIVING, LOVING & LEARNING," many others, by Leo F. Buscaglia, pub. by *Ballantine Books*, div. *Random House*, 201 E. 50th St., NY, NY 10022

"RICHES WITHIN YOUR REACH" by Robert Collier, pub. by *MacMillan & Co.*, 866 Third Ave., NY, NY 10022

"SCIENCE & HEALTH, WITH KEY TO THE SCRIPTURES" by Mary Baker Eddy, pub. by *Chrsitian Science Board of Directors*, 175 Huntington Ave., Boston, MA 02115

"TEN DAYS TO A GREAT NEW LIFE" by William E. Edwards, pub. by *Wilshire Book Co.*, 12015 Sherman Road, N. Hollywood, CA 91605

"THE DYNAMICS OF SUCCESSFUL ATTITUDES" by Bob Conklin, pub. by *Ballantine Books*, div. of *Random House*, 201 E. 50th St., NY, NY 10022

"THE POWER OF POSITIVE THINKING" by Norman Vincient Peale, Pub. by *Prentice-Hall*, 70 Fifth Avenue, NY, NY 10011

"THE POWER OF YOUR SUBCONSCIOUS MIND" by Dr. Joseph Murphy, pub. by *Parker Publshing Company*, West Nyack, NY 10994

"THE ULTIMATE SECRETS OF TOTAL SELF-CONFIDENCE" by Dr. Robert Anthony, pub. by *Berkeley Pub. Group*, 200 Madison Avenue, NY, NY 10016

TOASTMASTERS INTERNATIONAL, PO Box 9052, Mission Viejo, CA 92690

"WORD POWER" by Vernon Howard, pub. by *Prentice-Hall, Inc.*, Englewood Cliffs, NJ 07632

"YOU CAN HAVE IT ALL" by Arnold L. Patent, pub. by *Celebration Pub.*, Box 336, Piermont, NY 10968

"YOU HAVE ONE LIFE - GIVE IT YOUR BEST SHOT!" by Richard S. Clarke, pub. by *Exposition Press*, 900 South Oyster Bay Road, Hicksville, NY 11801